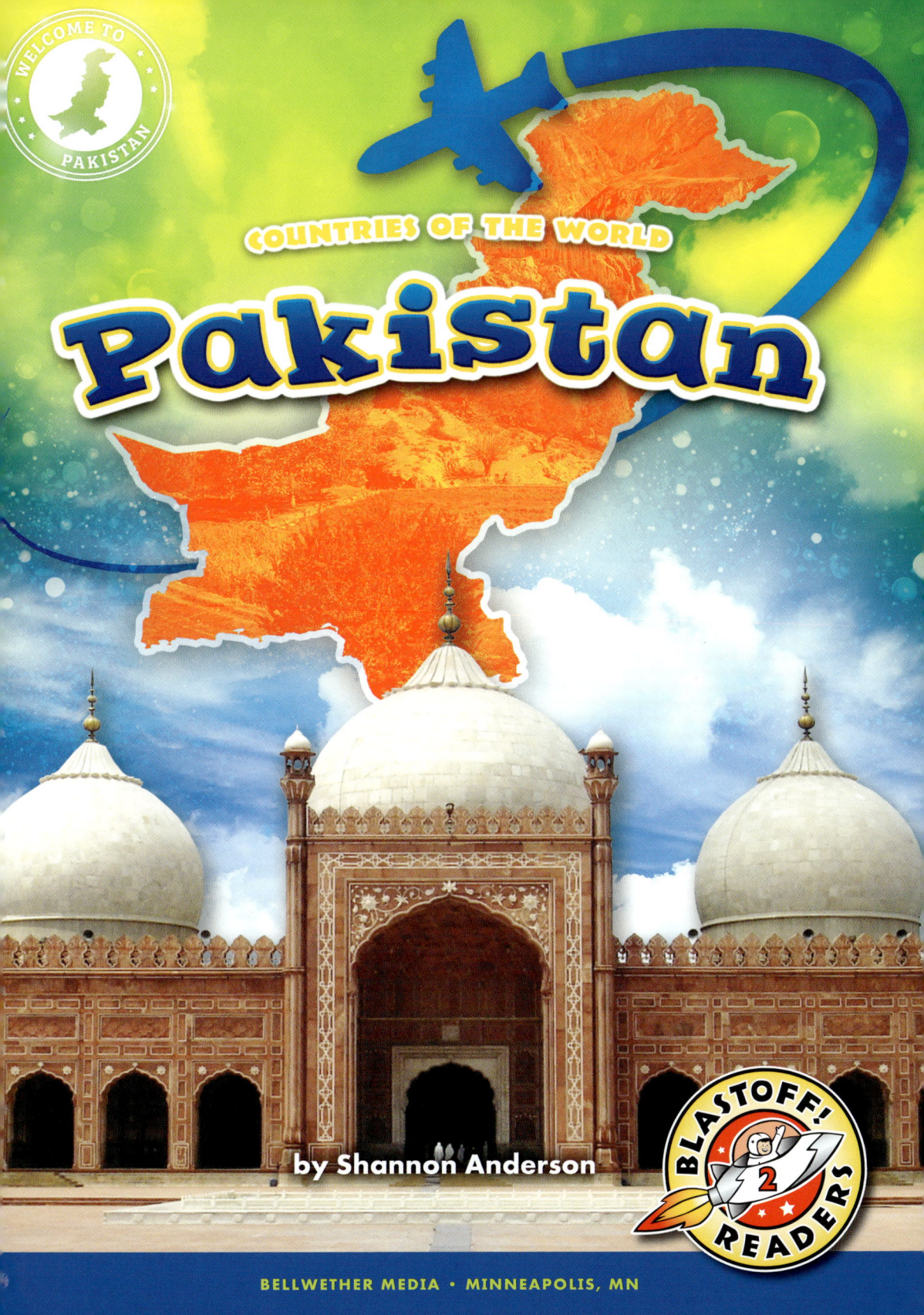

Blastoff! Readers are carefully developed by literacy experts to build reading stamina and move students toward fluency by combining standards-based content with developmentally appropriate text.

Level 1 provides the most support through repetition of high-frequency words, light text, predictable sentence patterns, and strong visual support.

Level 2 offers early readers a bit more challenge through varied sentences, increased text load, and text-supportive special features.

Level 3 advances early-fluent readers toward fluency through increased text load, less reliance on photos, advancing concepts, longer sentences, and more complex special features.

★ **Blastoff! Universe**

This edition first published in 2024 by Bellwether Media, Inc.

No part of this publication may be reproduced in whole or in part without written permission of the publisher. For information regarding permission, write to Bellwether Media, Inc., Attention: Permissions Department, 6012 Blue Circle Drive, Minnetonka, MN 55343.

Library of Congress Cataloging-in-Publication Data

LC record for Pakistan available at: https://lccn.loc.gov/2023046592

Text copyright © 2024 by Bellwether Media, Inc. BLASTOFF! READERS and associated logos are trademarks and/or registered trademarks of Bellwether Media, Inc.

Editor: Rachael Barnes   Designer: Gabriel Hilger

Printed in the United States of America, North Mankato, MN.

Table of Contents

All About Pakistan	4
Land and Animals	6
Life in Pakistan	12
Pakistan Facts	20
Glossary	22
To Learn More	23
Index	24

All About Pakistan

Islamabad

Pakistan is a large country in South Asia. Its capital is Islamabad.

The country is home to some of the world's tallest mountains!

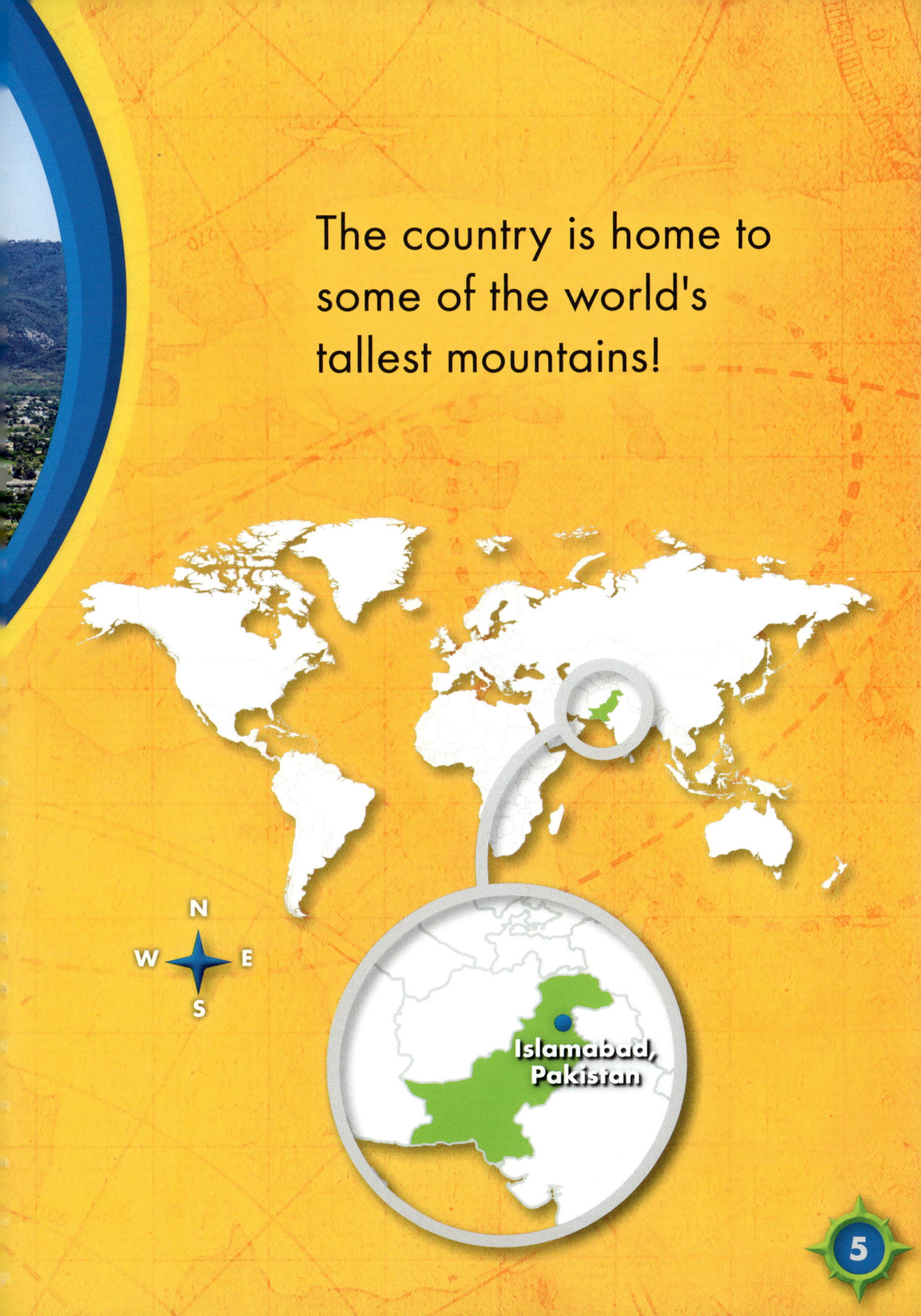

Land and Animals

Pakistan has many **deserts**. A large **plateau** covers the west. Mountains run through the country's center.

The Indus River flows through **plains** in the east. Beaches line the southern coast.

Indus River

K2

Size: 28,251 feet (8,611 meters) tall

Famous For: the world's second-tallest mountain

desert

Southern Pakistan is hot. It is colder in the north and in the mountains.

The country is often dry. But **monsoons** bring rain. The rain causes floods.

flood

Kingfishers catch fish in the Indus River. Honey badgers hunt in deserts.

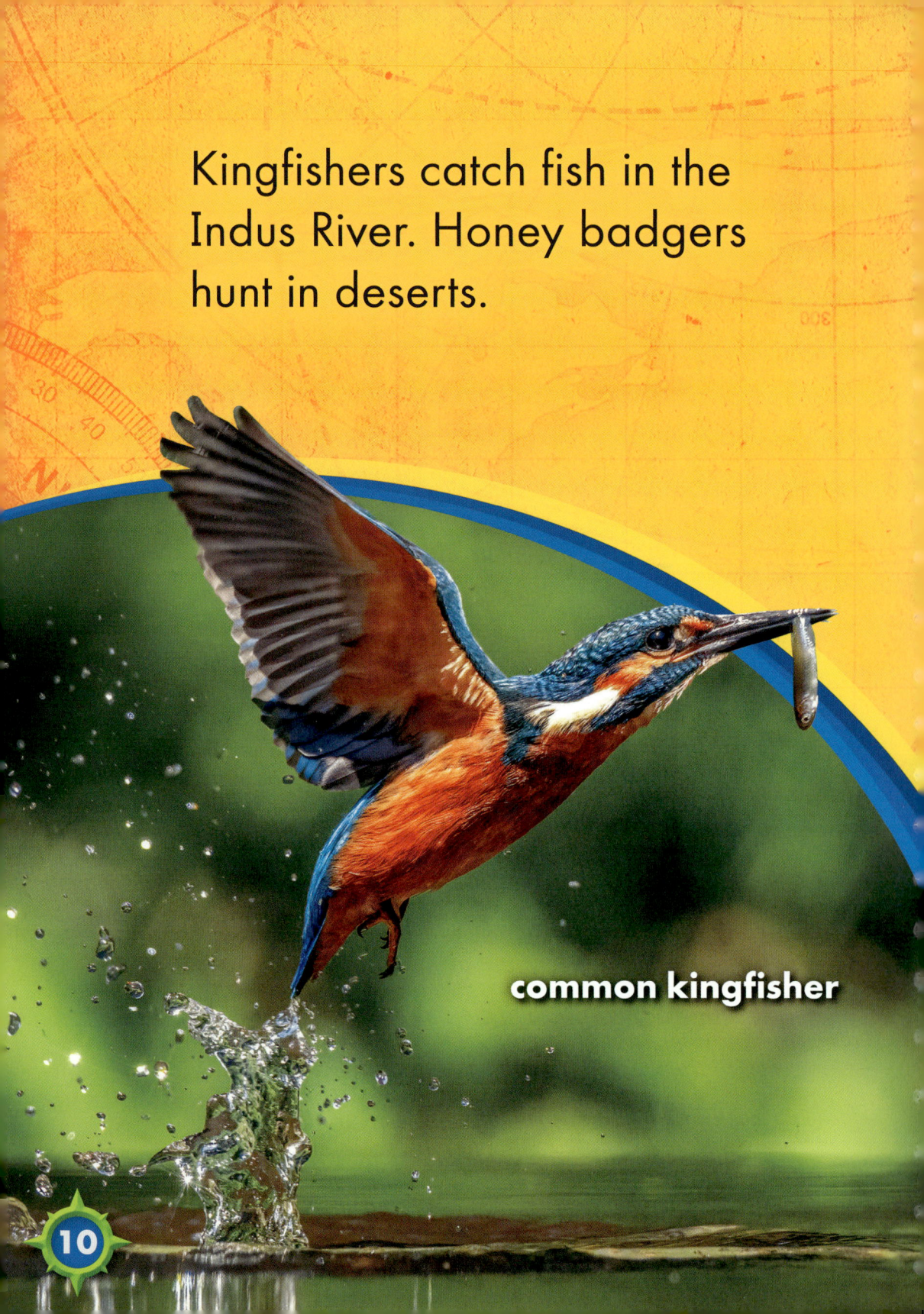

common kingfisher

Markhors live up in the mountains. Cobras climb in nearby trees.

Life in Pakistan

Most Pakistanis are **Muslims**. Many people live in small villages. About half of all Pakistanis have a **Punjabi** background.

Pakistan's official languages are Urdu and English. But many languages are spoken.

village

cricket

field hockey

Cricket is the most popular sport. Field hockey and soccer are other favorites.

Many people enjoy a game called *ludo*. Some attend poetry concerts. Poems are read out loud.

ludo

Flatbread is a **staple** food. It is served with *chai* for breakfast.

Pakistani Foods

flatbread

chai

sajji

biryani

making *chai*

Sajji is a lamb or chicken dish. *Biryani* is made with spiced rice and meat.

Pakistan Day is on March 23.
People go to parades.
They wave Pakistan's flag.

Eid al-Fitr

Muslims feast and pray during *Eid al-Fitr*. Families come together to **celebrate**!

Pakistan Facts

Size:
307,374 square miles
(796,095 square kilometers)

Population:
247,653,551 (2023)

National Holiday:
Pakistan Day (March 23)

Main Languages:
Urdu and English

Capital City:
Islamabad

Famous Face

Name: Yasmeen Lari
Famous For: Pakistan's first female architect who creates helpful buildings for communities in need

Religions

Muslim 97%   other 3%

Top Landmarks

Badshahi Mosque

Deosai National Park

Khewra Salt Mine

Glossary

celebrate—to do something special or fun for an event, occasion, or holiday

deserts—dry lands with few plants and little rainfall

monsoons—winds that shift direction each season; monsoons bring heavy rain.

Muslims—people of the Islamic faith; Muslims follow the teachings of Muhammad as told to him from Allah.

plains—large areas of flat land

plateau—a flat, raised area of land

Punjabi—related to people from the Punjab area in northwestern India

staple—a widely used food or other item

To Learn More

AT THE LIBRARY

Spanier, Kristine. *Pakistan*. Minneapolis, Minn.: Jump!, 2021.

Streza, Nancy. *Cricket*. Houston, Tex.: Xist Publishing, 2019.

Van, R.L. *Pakistan*. Minneapolis, Minn.: Abdo Publishing, 2023.

ON THE WEB

FACTSURFER

Factsurfer.com gives you a safe, fun way to find more information.

1. Go to www.factsurfer.com.

2. Enter "Pakistan" into the search box and click 🔍.

3. Select your book cover to see a list of related content.

Index

animals, 10, 11
beaches, 6
capital (see Islamabad)
coast, 6
cricket, 14
deserts, 6, 8, 10
Eid al-Fitr, 19
English, 12
field hockey, 14
floods, 9
food, 16, 17
Indus River, 6, 10
Islamabad, 4, 5
K2, 7
ludo, 15
map, 5
monsoons, 9
mountains, 5, 6, 7, 8, 11
Muslims, 12, 19

Pakistan Day, 18
Pakistan facts, 20–21
people, 12, 15, 18, 19
plains, 6
plateau, 6
poetry, 15
Punjabi, 12
rain, 9
say hello, 13
soccer, 14
South Asia, 4
Urdu, 12, 13
villages, 12

The images in this book are reproduced through the courtesy of: Matej Hudovernik, front cover; Mairee992, pp. 2-3; Dmitrii Shirinkin, p. 3 (flag); thsulemani, pp. 4-5; iamnuang, p. 6; khlongwangchao, pp. 6-7; Nadeem A. Khan, pp. 8-9; Kamran Khan, p. 9; Albert Beaukhof, pp. 10-11; WildMedia, p. 11 (common kingfisher); Pavel Kovaricek, p. 11 (honey badger); Popova Valeriya, p. 11 (markhor); Omid Mozaffari/ Wiki Commons, p. 11 (Central Asian cobra); Nataliia Milko, p. 12; Syed Fahad Hussain Shah, pp. 12-13; Jahanzaib Naiyyer, p. 14 (cricket); mooinblack, p. 14 (field hockey); Asianet-Pakistan, p. 15 (*ludo*); Santhosh Varghese, p. 16 (flatbread, *biryani*); AlafStudio, p. 16 (*chai*); Fanfo, p. 16 (*sajji*); maazrafy, p. 17; zubair abbasi, pp. 18-19; titoOnz, p. 20 (flag); BBC Urdu/ Wiki Commons, p. 20 (Yasmeen Lari); suronin, p. 21 (Badshahi Mosque); Sarosh Akram Qureshi, p. 21 (Deosai National Park); Bay_Media, p. 21 (Khewra Salt Mine); Christopher Chambers, p. 22.